Co-operative Tax Compliance

BUILDING BETTER TAX CONTROL FRAMEWORKS

This work is published under the responsibility of the Secretary-General of the OECD. The opinions expressed and arguments employed herein do not necessarily reflect the official views of OECD member countries.

Please cite this publication as:
OECD (2016), *Co-operative Tax Compliance: Building Better Tax Control Frameworks*, OECD Publishing, Paris.
http://dx.doi.org/10.1787/9789264253384-en

ISBN 978-92-64-25398-8 (print)
ISBN 978-92-64-25338-4 (PDF)

The statistical data for Israel are supplied by and under the responsibility of the relevant Israeli authorities. The use of such data by the OECD is without prejudice to the status of the Golan Heights, East Jerusalem and Israeli settlements in the West Bank under the terms of international law.

Table of contents

Abbreviations and acronyms

BIAC	Business and Industry Advisory Committee
BEPS	Base erosion and profit shifting
COSO	Committee on Sponsoring Organisations of the Treadway Commission
DOTAS	Disclosure of Tax Avoidance Schemes
FASB	Financial Accounting Standards Board
FTA	Forum on Tax Administration
ICS	Internal control statement
LBP	Large Business Programme
OECD	Organisation for Economic Co-operation and Development
SAO	Senior Accounting Officer
TCF	Tax Control Framework
UK	United Kingdom
USA	United States of America
VAT	Value added tax

Executive summary

A Tax Control Framework (TCF) is the part of the system of internal control that assures the accuracy and completeness of the tax returns and disclosures made by an enterprise. The TCF plays a central part in bringing rigour to the co-operative compliance concept.

This report has been prepared by the OECD's Forum on Tax Administration's Large Business Programme (FTA LBP), which is a network of experts on large business taxation. It is the result of work undertaken by those experts following the publication of the FTA report Co-operative Compliance: A Framework – From Enhanced Relationship to Co-operative Compliance (the "2013 report", OECD, 2013a) in May 2013. The content of the guide has benefited from discussion with members of the tax committee of the Business and Industry Advisory Committee to the OECD (BIAC) and with members of the large accounting firms that advise multinational enterprises.

The objective of this report is to provide guidance that is meant to be helpful for businesses to design and operate their TCFs and for revenue bodies to adjust the risk management strategy for an individual large business in the context of a (voluntary) co-operative compliance relationship as laid out in the FTA report Study into the Role of Tax Intermediaries (OECD, 2008), the 2013 report, and the September 2013 BIAC Statement of Tax Principles for International Business (see Annex A).

The broad conclusions of this report are that when the tax control framework of a multinational enterprise participating in cooperative compliance programme is determined to be effective, and when the enterprise provides complete disclosures that include relevant information and tax risks and is transparent to the revenue body, the extent of reviews and audits of the returns submitted to it can be reduced significantly. In these circumstances, the revenue body may rely on the returns submitted to it and trust that uncertain tax positions and other problematic tax positions taken in that return will be brought to its attention.

Based on these conclusions, and building on the work of the Large Business Programme and of the Forum on Tax Administration, this report recommends that:

1. In relation to member countries concerned about evaluating the risk management systems, structures and policies of businesses that have committed to engage in a co-operative compliance relationship they should:
   - Review the content of this report with a view to evaluating how these TCFs can best be assessed
   - Leverage TCFs to continue finding ways to strengthen the cooperative compliance model through effective management of compliance risks including providing certainty in exchange for transparency

2. In relation to evaluating risk management systems, this report recommends that FTA countries:

   – Formulate their own methods of evaluating businesses risk management systems

3. In relation to obtaining greater assurance about the reliability of these systems from a tax perspective this report recommends that FTA countries:

   – Evaluate the merits of issuing additional guidance designed to ensure the disclosure of tax risks.

Chapter 1

Introduction

This chapter provides background information on the OECD's work on co-operative compliance and outlines how the Tax Control Framework can play a central role in successfully implementing this concept.

Background

This guide has been prepared by the OECD's Forum on Tax Administration's Large Business Programme (FTA LBP), which is a network of experts on large business taxation. It is the result of work undertaken by those experts following the publication of the FTA report *Co-operative Compliance: A Framework – From Enhanced Relationship to Co-operative Compliance* (the "2013 report", OECD, 2013a) in May 2013. The content of the guide has benefited from discussion with members of the tax committee of the Business and Industry Advisory Committee to the OECD (BIAC) and with members of the large accounting firms that advise multinational enterprises.

The first recommendation of the 2013 report reads as follows:

> *Given the central importance of Tax Control Frameworks (TCF) there is a need for more research and discussion of how these frameworks can best be assessed and what additional guidance could be given to business about revenue bodies' expectations of them.*

In order to follow up all the recommendations of the 2013 Report, a meeting of the FTA's network of experts on large business taxation, representing 30 revenue bodies, was held in Paris on 17-19 February, 2014. The meeting was also attended by representatives of BIAC, leading accounting firms, and some of the external oversight bodies that audit the operations of tax administrations. During the first day of this meeting the topic of the TCF was discussed in depth, and a detailed record of the discussions was prepared and agreed by the attendees. It was decided that a smaller task team of countries would work with representatives of BIAC and the Accountancy profession to develop the thinking about the TCF in more detail. Delegates from the revenue bodies of Australia, Canada, Finland, France, Mexico, the Netherlands, Spain, Sweden, Switzerland, the United Kingdom and the United States, and representatives from BIAC and the Accountancy profession met in Den Bosch, in the Netherlands, on 19 November 2014 for that purpose. This guide is a synthesis of the conclusions reached during these two meetings and in subsequent written exchanges.

The 2013 report took stock of developments in the application of the concept of co-operative compliance and the changes that have taken place in the business and economic environment since the publication of the FTA's *Study into the Role of Tax Intermediaries* (the "2008 report", OECD, 2008). Co-operative compliance programs are designed to establish on a voluntary basis a relationship based on co-operation and trust between businesses and revenue bodies. The 2013 Report sets out the benefits that Co-operative Compliance programmes can deliver both for tax administrations and for large businesses that participate.

One of the conclusions in the report identified the tax control framework (TCF) as centrally important to effective Co-operative Compliance programmes:

> *Basing the relationship on an explicit and objective assessment of the taxpayer's ability and willingness to provide the necessary disclosure and transparency (the TCF) means that it is and can be seen to be based on justified trust and empirical evidence.*

The TCF plays a central part in bringing rigour to the co-operative compliance concept. It is important that within multinational enterprises participating in cooperative compliance programmes, senior managers, up to and including board-level executives, understand:

- the purpose and importance of the TCF;
- their responsibility to be in control of tax risks; and
- the agreement to be transparent with revenue bodies.

It is equally important that revenue bodies at all levels recognize that a) where it has determined that the tax control framework of a multinational enterprise participating in cooperative compliance programme is effective; and b) the enterprise provides complete disclosures that include relevant information and tax risks and is transparent to the revenue body, the extent of reviews and audits of the returns submitted to it can be reduced significantly. This is mutually beneficial to both multinational enterprises and revenue bodies and by extension, society as a whole.

In these circumstances the revenue body may rely on the returns submitted to it and trust that uncertain tax positions and other problematic tax positions taken in that return will be brought to its attention. This common understanding about a TCF, its essential features, and how it is deployed in practice underpin the successful operation of a co-operative compliance relationship. To assure external stakeholders, including the public, that the revenue body is impartial, tax officials must remain impartial and professional, and maintain independence in attitude in all matters relating to the taxpayer and the information and tax risks that it discloses.

This guide has three main elements. Chapter 2 outlines the essential features of a TCF and so addresses what revenue bodies' expectations of TCFs are. It includes a discussion of the issue of materiality, as it is important to understand the relationship between what is material for the purposes of systems of control, such as the external audit of a multinational enterprise's accounts, and what is material in terms of the tax liabilities arising from that enterprise's activities in a particular country. Chapter 3 discusses how revenue bodies could approach the task of testing the soundness of a TCF in any particular case. Chapter 4 sets out conclusions, recommendations and next steps.

Scope of this guidance

It is worth emphasising that this guidance is just that; it should not be viewed as prescriptive. It is meant to be helpful for businesses to design and operate their TCFs and for revenue bodies to adjust the risk management strategy for an individual large business in the context of a (voluntary) co-operative compliance relationship as laid out in the FTA report *Study into the Role of Tax Intermediaries* (OECD, 2008), the 2013 report and in the September 2013 BIAC Statement of Tax Principles for International Business (see Annex A). This guidance does not introduce additional rights or obligations between taxpayers and tax administrations.

Countries that have implemented the cooperative compliance concept have adapted it to operate within the broader context of their country's tax system, administrative practice and culture. Therefore it should be recognised that there are differences between revenue bodies, with resulting different 'starting positions'. Equally, multinational enterprises by definition operate in many different jurisdictions and the practical application of the ideas discussed here may need to vary to take into account the specific requirements of individual countries. This means that it is not possible to develop a "one–size-fits-all" guide. However, the guide does adopt a "top down" approach, which is to say that it assumes that the essential features of a TCF will be determined at the top level of the enterprise (i.e. senior management), rather than being an amalgamation of individual decisions made lower down in the organisation about what controls are needed.

It is important to note that since the release of the 2013 Report (OECD, 2013a) for which this body of work represents follow-up guidance, the international tax landscape has changed significantly with the development and adoption of the comprehensive OECD/G20 Action Plan on Base Erosion and Profit Shifting (BEPS) (OECD, 2013b). The BEPS initiative represented a bold move by policy makers to restore confidence in the system and ensure that profits are taxed where economic activities take place and value is created. It was undertaken to restore trust of ordinary people in the fairness of their tax systems, to level the playing field among businesses, and to further enhance transparency and coordination between tax administrations. The package of BEPS Actions included new or reinforced international standards as well as concrete measures to help countries tackle BEPS. BEPS will also improve the information available to tax authorities to apply their tax laws effectively. As a result of BEPS, it has become even more crucial for multinational enterprises to be in control of tax risks today than when the 2013 Report was written, which thereby further amplifies the significance that an effective tax control framework provides as an essential component of a business's tax risk management practice.

Chapter 2

The essential features of a Tax Control Framework

This chapter outlines the essential features of a Tax Control Framework (TCF) and addresses revenue bodies' expectations. It also discusses the application of TCFs and the issue of materiality.

The importance of the TCF lies in its ability to provide a verifiable assurance that the information and returns submitted by a taxpayer are both accurate and complete. At one level, there is nothing novel in this. Taxpayers have always been obliged to submit accurate tax returns. However, co-operative compliance places an additional emphasis on disclosure and transparency. Disclosure signifies the willingness of the taxpayer to make the revenue body aware of any tax positions taken in the return that may be uncertain or controversial, and being ready to go beyond their statutory obligations to disclose. Transparency refers to sharing information about the internal control system, including the design, implementation and effectiveness of the TCF that enables the taxpayer to be fully aware and "in control" of all the positions and issues that need to be disclosed. The integrity and robustness of a well-designed and effective TCF that has been tested by the revenue body is empirical evidence that underpins the "justified" trust in a taxpayer, and in return the revenue body can provide certainty on the disclosed tax positions.

The 2013 Report describes the TCF as "The part of the system of internal control that assures the accuracy and completeness of the tax returns and disclosures made by an enterprise is sometimes referred to as the Tax Control Framework." (OECD, 2013a).[1] Almost all Corporate Governance legislation or codes oblige the boards of enterprises to issue an "Internal Control Statement" (ICS). The ICS is concerned with the Enterprise Risk Management System of the enterprise. Chapter 4 of the 2013 report discusses the relationship between the overall system for internal control and the TCF, which is an integral part of that overall system. It follows that the TCF should be built up starting from the basic thinking about internal control.

The OECD recently published Corporate Governance and Business Integrity,[2] a report that highlights the extent to which companies are organising themselves in order to integrate considerations of business integrity into their corporate governance frameworks, strategy, and operations. This report references the updated G20/OECD Principles of Corporate Governance,[3] a set of specific recommendations on the role of the board and executive management in setting the ethical tone in a company and exercising oversight of its business integrity policies. Additionally, the OECD Guidelines for Multinational Enterprises published in 2011 included recommendations for enterprises to treat tax governance and tax compliance as important elements of their oversight and broader risk management systems.[4]

Individual enterprises base their systems of internal control on principles such as those cited in the OECD reports and in frameworks such as that of the Committee of Sponsoring Organisations of the Treadway Commission (known as COSO). However, the specifics of the system of internal control have to reflect the particular circumstances of the business and industry in question. Consequently, it is not possible to prescribe a one-size-fits-all system of control for all enterprises. Similarly, this guide does not attempt to prescribe a one-size-fits-all TCF. Instead, the discussions on which this guide is based have identified six essential building blocks of a TCF.

Essential building blocks of a TCF

Six principles or essential building blocks were identified. They are consistent with existing enterprise-wide models of internal control such as COSO, and can be summarised as follows:

- **Tax Strategy Established**: This should be clearly documented and owned by the senior management of the enterprise, i.e. at Board level;

- **Applied Comprehensively**: All transactions entered into by an enterprise are capable of affecting its tax position in one way or another, which means that the TCF needs to be able to govern the full range of the enterprise's activities and ideally should be embedded in day to day management of business operations;

- **Responsibility Assigned**: The board of an enterprise is accountable for the design, implementation and effectiveness of the tax control framework of that enterprise. The role of the enterprise's tax department and its responsibility for the implementation of the TCF should be clearly recognised and properly resourced;

- **Governance Documented**: There needs to be a system of rules and reporting that ensures transactions and events are compared with the expected norms and potential risks of non-compliance identified and managed. This governance process should be explicitly documented and sufficient resources deployed to implement the TCF and review its effectiveness periodically.

- **Testing Performed**: Compliance with the policies and processes embodied in the TCF should be the subject of regular monitoring, testing and maintenance.

- **Assurance Provided**: The tax control framework should be capable of providing assurance to stakeholders, including external stakeholders such as a tax administration, that tax risks are subject to proper control and that outputs such as tax returns can be relied upon. This is accomplished by establishing the entity's "risk appetite" and then by ensuring that their Risk Management Framework is capable of identifying departures from that with mechanisms for mitigating/eliminating the additional risk.

These building blocks are generic in nature. In certain specific industry sectors they may need to be supplemented with some additional features that reflect the particular risks associated with those industries. This guide does not attempt to address these industry specific aspects of TCFs.

The final building block (**Assurance Provided**) can be seen as the overall result of having put in place all the other building blocks; if they are there it is possible to provide the desired assurance. The way in which an enterprise will communicate that assurance will depend on the particular regulatory climate in which it operates and its overall risk management strategy, including its communication strategy. It is recognised that there may be differences in the level of effectiveness at which the various building blocks are performing, which should be an important element of the discussion between the enterprise and tax administration. The other five building blocks merit some additional comment.

Tax Strategy Established

The TCF must reflect and document the tax strategy and the tax objectives of a business. A strategy can be defined as a plan of action designed to achieve a long-term or overall aim.[5] This plan of action should transparently display the overall tax strategy ranging from the strategic level to the operational level, including the tax risk strategy, risk appetite, the board's degree of engagement with tax planning decisions, reporting, filing and payment strategies. The tax strategy should also encompass the so called "tone at the top" or soft controls and should clearly articulate the board's risk appetite. The TCF should include objectives covering risk management processes, clear objectives with respect to opportunities such as tax planning opportunities, clear objectives in terms of what is to be expected or achieved, and a strategy for using technology to maximise the quality and accuracy of the data that underpins the tax return and associated declarations.

The tax strategy will reflect business's appetite for risk, which includes its willingness to adopt tax positions that the relevant revenue body may disagree with. Does the appetite for risk say something about the robustness of an enterprise's TCF? There is a distinction to be made here between high risk taxpayers (with inherent risks that may arise because of the complexity of their business transactions, the industry sector or a combination of the two) and high risk behaviour (appetite for risk). It was agreed that it is possible to have a high risk taxpayer in a co-operative compliance relationship if the behavioural risks of that taxpayer are low. Disclosure (the willingness to disclose up-front those positions that may concern the revenue body) and transparency (being in control) are critical to maintaining relationships in such situations.

A tax strategy should include certain elements, such as an operational roadmap, the objectives and measures of the business, how the organisation, tax department and objectives are steered and a statement that the business complies with the law. Chapter three of the *Co-operative Compliance: A Framework – From Enhanced Relationship to Co-operative Compliance* report (OECD, 2013a) discusses in detail a taxpayer's compliance with the spirit of the law and also concludes that transparency is key in a co-operative compliance relationship. It specifically recognises that a taxpayer may legitimately have a different view from the revenue body about the correct treatment of a (tax) position taken; the essential point being that in a co-operative compliance relationship the taxpayer will be completely open about the position it has adopted. As stated in the 2013 Report:

> *It is only possible to have an effective discussion about the interpretation of the law if all facts are clear and accepted by both parties. Within a co-operative relationship the parties try to obtain a common understanding of all the relevant facts and circumstances in order to speed up the process and resolve disputes quicker.*[6]

Applied Comprehensively

To be comprehensive a TCF should adopt a process-oriented approach in which all tax policy, rules, procedures and processes within the business are documented for all relevant taxes, including the identified (soft) controls and identified process owners (as envisaged under the Sarbanes-Oxley Act). The TCF should reflect the tax strategy objectives of the business and whether the processes deliver these goals. The TCF needs to identify the tax treatment during the whole process (i.e. from strategy through to monitoring/testing and from planning the transaction through to implementation). It should cover routine transactions and allow for identifying non-routine transactions. To deliver on its role as a central part in bringing rigour to the cooperative compliance concept, the TCF must also include clear processes to identify and disclose privileged communication such as opinions and advice about tax positions taken in the return that may be uncertain or controversial.

Responsibility Assigned

The development of the tax strategy and the TCF is the responsibility of senior management which includes the incorporation of the tax strategy in the TCF and approval by the CFO/Board. For a successful implementation of a tax strategy it is critical that it is executed by people who have the right skills and experience. The execution of the tax strategy is the main responsibility of the tax department, but it should be recognised that tax functions could also sit outside the tax department.

Box 2.1. Example – TCF Guidance from the Netherlands

Guidance provided for large business by the Netherlands Tax and Customs Administration, states that, "The organisation has designed its tax control framework in a manner that ensures that it is aware of all relevant events with consequences for taxation. This requires communication structures to be employed by the officers (i.e. management and other operational staff) bearing tax responsibilities. Examples include forms of consultation that discuss financial, legal and operational events and which involve the officer bearing the tax responsibility. This is necessary as the organisation needs to identify risks. The tax risks are then assessed and, where relevant, action is taken to control those risks.[7]"

Source: Netherlands Tax and Customs Administration

Governance Documented

Business should also have tax governance that is aligned with the business and tax strategy reflecting the expectations of customers, clients, staff, shareholders and other stakeholders.

> *Tax governance and tax compliance are important elements of the broader risk management system. Corporate boards should adopt tax risk management strategies to ensure that the financial, regulatory and reputational risks are fully identified and evaluated. The commitment of businesses to co-operate, to be transparent and to be tax compliant should be reflected in its risk management systems, structures and policies. A comprehensive risk management strategy that includes tax will allow the enterprise to act as a good corporate citizen but also to effectively manage tax risk.* (OECD, 2013a)[8]

Corporate governance deals with the rights and responsibilities of a business's board, senior executives, management and employees, shareholders and other stakeholders. Good corporate governance reflects how well a business is run and it affects the business performance and market confidence in the business. On the other hand poor corporate governance can result in high risk such as non-compliance.

A satisfactory TCF should reflect good tax governance starting with the alignment of the risk committee of a business's Board with clear written tax governance policies. Business risk committees are generally responsible for overseeing all risks and risk related activities other than those undertaken by the Board or other Board committees. For example, in some corporations the Audit Committee oversees tax and accounting risks, and the full Board governs strategic and reputational risks. The tax governance process should describe and define for example all tax responsibilities, the accountability, the key performance indicators (KPIs), communication methods, a correct definition of materiality for tax purposes, monitoring and mitigating of tax risks and testing of the TCF.

Another key feature in the governance process is the board level sign-off. The purpose of board level sign-off is to declare at the highest level that the business is in control of its tax processes - the TCF is designed to be operationally effective (the processes that have been established are followed in practice), maintained and monitored. Through the sign-off, the board is expressly confirming that the key elements of a tax control framework, such as those articulated earlier in this chapter for example, are in working order and effective. Signing off is also a means for the business to have ongoing discussions about internal control risk management, being in control and transparent, and to keep responsibility for tax in the boardroom. The value of signing off lies in the explicit statement that the business is committed to the specific process designed to realise in practice the principle commitment to transparency. A properly functioning TCF is a prerequisite for creating justified trust between the business and the tax administration. For the business, signing off is a means of declaring that it has done its due diligence and that it has taken all necessary steps to be in control. Sign-off should occur at the end of the cycle and/or annually by the CFO or senior accounting officer (SAO). Examples of how sign off can be given is by signing off for example the TCF itself, the tax return, the co-operative compliance agreement, the Internal Control Framework and the Internal Control Statement.

Testing Performed

Testing the TCF should combine the monitoring process with maintenance of the framework. The monitoring component should contain feedback tools and solutions to detect and correct errors and improve the TCF so that any errors are not repeated. Maintenance should take place on a regular basis and following any fundamental changes to the business, such as changes in the business strategy, in the board, in the tax department, in tax legislation, in the business structure or model, in the supply chain, and following major acquisitions or disposals. Monitoring the TCF is the responsibility of business; however as discussed in Chapter 3 - *Testing Tax Control: Frameworks*, (OECD, 2013a)[9] the revenue body should conduct real-time testing in order to assure itself that the TCF is functioning and producing the expected outcomes.

Access to data

When it comes to the practical application of the TCF to the management of complex tax issues and disputes about them, it was recognised that access to good quality and relevant data is critically important. It was also recognised that this was often the source of considerable friction in the relationship between taxpayers and revenue bodies. Taxpayers sometimes feel that information requests go well beyond what is relevant and give rise to avoidable costs and unnecessary delay. Revenue bodies may feel compelled to act if they believe they are being denied access to primary documentation, or deliberately drowned in documentation, most of which is not relevant to the issue in question.

In the context of a co-operative compliance relationship there should be much less scope for disagreement about the facts and the TCF has an important part to play in ensuring that this is the case. For example, the application of an effective TCF to a particular transaction should mean that the tax issues it gives rise to are clearly documented and the relevant documentation is readily available. It helps that the co-operative compliance approach usually means that discussions of key transactions will generally take place much closer to the time of execution, when access to the relevant documents and decision makers is much easier to arrange. This is one of the key ways in which co-operative compliance delivers earlier and greater certainty to both parties at lower cost.

The issue of materiality

Materiality is a significant issue in the context of TCFs. Materiality as defined for the purposes of the external audit undertaken on behalf of shareholders is generally defined as "The omission or misstatement of an item in a financial report is material if, in the light of surrounding circumstances, the magnitude of the item is such that it is probable that the judgment of a reasonable person relying upon the report would have been changed or influenced by the inclusion or correction of the item." (FASB, 2008) Given the purpose of the external audit, this is a perfectly reasonable test, but it is not one that would work in deciding what is material for tax purposes. If materiality is determined at the level of the overall economic entity, in some instances what is material will be a number that exceeds the total tax payable by that entity in a particular country.

The concept of materiality in the context of TCFs is a complex one and no single approach can be recommended. TCFs should be designed and implemented to prevent, detect and correct errors. An essential and integrated part of the TCF is the testing and monitoring of its adequacy. Materiality is a variable that can be used, by analogy with audit, to determine the workload (volume and intensity) of testing and monitoring. In general, two aspects of materiality can be recognized. Firstly, materiality can be applied as a nominal value, a fixed monetary amount. Secondly, some omissions or misstatements are material by their nature, like fraud, irrespective of the magnitude in terms of monetary value.

Other suggestions for determining the issue of materiality include looking at the company code, which may say something about the risk categorisation, staffing, compliance risks, and the nature of compliance behaviour and/or by discussing what is material for the taxpayer.

Box 2.2. Example - Defining materiality

In the Netherlands, the first aspect of materiality is called quantitative materiality and the second, qualitative materiality. The Netherlands uses a quantitative materiality determined as a fixed amount, which depends on the size of the organisation - of the (Dutch) turnover. Qualitative materiality refers to the significance of an identified (and, consequently, known) misstatement and, in particular, the nature of the misstatement. The nature primarily relates to the degree of culpability for the misstatement. (Serious) culpability for a misstatement in the Netherlands will always lead to adjustments of a tax return, even when the financial consequences are (relatively) small.

Source: Netherlands Tax and Customs Administration

Notes

1. See Chapter 4 - The importance of the Tax Control Framework, page 58.
2. www.oecd.org/daf/ca/Corporate-Governance-Business-Integrity-2015.pdf
3. www.oecd.org/daf/ca/Corporate-Governance-Principles-ENG.pdf
4. www.oecd.org/corporate/mne/48004323.pdf
5. www.oxforddictionaries.com/definition/english/strategy
6. See page 52.
7. http://download.belastingdienst.nl/itd/beleid/overige/tax_control_framework.pdf
8. See page 57.
9. See page 57.

Chapter 3

Assessing and testing Tax Control Frameworks

This chapter discusses how revenue bodies could approach the task of testing the soundness of a TCF operated by an enterprise.

Assessing the TCF

In order for revenue bodies to gain assurance that the TCF operated by an enterprise is both sound in principle and being followed in practice, they need to obtain knowledge and establish an understanding about what controls are in place. The assessment of the TCF can be undertaken by reference to the essential features discussed in Chapter 2. Revenue bodies may adopt different forms of assessment ranging from selective to substantive.

There are some specific approaches that revenue bodies could adopt to assess the TCF:

- *Question the management of the business*: A natural place to start is by asking management of the business to explain how the TCF works.

  – Focus on controls that are or should be in place, how these controls are tested and review all relevant documentation. The TCF should be aligned with the business operations.

  – Ask what the management did and ask for exception reports and for details of the consequent actions taken. Who 'signed off' on a transaction? What is the communications system between tax and the rest of the business? What are the *consequences of not adhering* to the TCF for actors within the business?

  – Ask about the decision making process in case of an internal conflict and how the tax decisions are made (e.g. escalation to the CEO).

- Examine the changes that take place as a result of new legislation or business restructuring to test how the framework is working and look whether the framework is able to identify process failure/ errors. A TCF should make clear what happens if an error occurs, and a good TCF is evidence that errors are not the result of negligence.

- Other means of assessing the TCF include performing reality checks, auditing tax returns, and reviewing periodical reporting as well as examining the capability of the tax team, their tax skills, business awareness and inquiring about tools in place to assess the effectiveness of the framework. Also, looking at which indicators provide management knowledge and assurance that the controls are working, and what evidence the business has of independent evaluation of the framework could be built in the assessment process.

If the revenue body comes to the conclusion that a business does not have an appropriate TCF, the consequences for the business of not adhering to the obligation of having an appropriate framework should be clear for both the revenue body and for the business.

Testing the TCF

When it comes to testing the application of the TCF in practice, revenue bodies need to leverage their explicit understanding of what the process for managing risks is as determined through their assessment of the TCF, and they should ascertain for themselves how effective it is by testing it themselves. Testing provides revenue bodies the opportunity to gain insight into how the business delivers compliance and therefore it provides them comfort that the risks are managed properly. Revenue bodies should stay "in contact" with the process in order to define relevant milestones.

To assist with the maintenance of the TCF, taxpayers would benefit from feedback from the tax administration's review which is fundamental for improving the TCF. It was agreed there is benefit in revenue bodies being transparent with business on potential tax risks, their view or assessment of the TCF, and, specifically, any areas where the tax administration has reservations about the level of control being achieved in practice. A business should have an appropriately designed and operationally effective TCF (that includes an effective monitoring function) to evidence the "justified trust" that is essential for a Co-operative Compliance relationship. Equally, revenue bodies also need to make clear to what extent they adjust their risk assessment of the business and their compliance activities in light of the scope and quality of the TCF.

Testing can have different forms ranging from substantive testing to testing of some particular aspects. Revenue bodies may select particular aspects for testing and maintain dialogue with the business about these aspects, the controls in place and the implications for their audit approach. Ultimately, a TCF must be designed in such a way to allow revenue bodies to determine whether it can provide assurance as to the reliability of the financial/tax statements and reports.

There are some specific approaches that revenue bodies can adopt in testing the adequacy of the TCF:

- *Controls should be in place*. As with any audit, check what controls exist within and outside the business such as controls from external auditors and other (competent) authorities, such as regulators. The revenue body's approach to assurance should aim to build on those pre-existing controls, for example examining how the business has tested for itself that the controls are effective and the audit trail and documentation created as a result. Revenue bodies could be transparent with the business about their approach to obtaining the assurance they need.

- *Managing execution risks*. Significant tax risks can arise in the process of execution, for example when changes to the specific structure, or sequencing of a transaction are made at the last moment as it is in the process of being implemented. The tax implications of these changes need to be controlled but there is a risk that this will not be the case. The TCF must detect and identify execution risks. Examining how the TCF is applied to manage execution risks in practice is a potentially important part of testing by a revenue body. Comparing, or "benchmarking" the ways in which different businesses do this may be helpful.

- Looking at what key changes have taken place in the company's operating environment and how effectively these have been reflected (e.g. detected, documented and reported) in the detail of the TCF. Relevant changes could include changes in tax legislation or business restructuring.

- Previous OECD FTA publications cited in Annex B of this report also provide additional information that can be taken into consideration for testing a TCF, including guidance relating to tax accounting systems and business and accounting software.

Assurance can also be provided by:

- Comparing economic performance of businesses such as industry based approaches to bring out common approaches.

- *Mandatory disclosure regimes.* To obtain greater assurance about the reliability of these systems from a tax perspective, revenue bodies in most OECD countries have issued additional guidance designed to ensure the disclosure of tax risks. As mentioned in the 2013 Report,

  "[t]he undertakings by businesses to provide full disclosure are often voluntary and part of a cooperative compliance programme (e.g. Australia, Austria, Ireland, The Netherlands, New Zealand, Singapore, South Africa and the USA). But several countries, including Canada, Ireland, South Africa the United States and the UK also have mandatory disclosure regimes. In the UK, the Tax Compliance Risk Management (TCRM) Framework and the Code of Practice on Taxation for Banks are underpinned by statutory penalties for failures to comply with Senior Accounting Officer (SAO) and Disclosure of Tax Avoidance Schemes (DOTAS) obligations. We have already mentioned that the USA and Australia also have specific statutory rules requiring the disclosure of uncertain tax positions. Overall, these disclosure regimes reinforce the need for good systems of internal control and provide revenue bodies with evidence that they can use to check the effectiveness of those systems."(OECD, 2013a)[1]

- For those revenue bodies that do not have mandatory disclosure regimes, Action 12 of BEPS (OECD, 2015a) provides a modular framework of guidance drawn from best practices for use by countries seeking to design such regimes in order to obtain early information on aggressive or abusive tax planning schemes and their users.

The TCF is a process that enables the management of the business to be in control regarding the tax risks making it possible to file complete and accurate tax returns. Consequently, a TCF does not provide an agreement about what the final tax bill will be. Assessing and testing the TCF are the means whereby the revenue body obtains assurance about the underlying reliability of the tax return and the accompanying disclosure of the material tax risks that arise from that return and the transactions it reflects. Businesses benefit when the required level of assurance is provided in this way, as it is possible to rapidly narrow down the issues for discussion during the tax assessment or audit process.

Errors may occur even in a cooperative compliance relationship that includes a well-developed, implemented and governed TCF. In these circumstances, a good TCF should be evidence that an error is not the result of some form of systemic negligence. Nevertheless, the revenue body will require assurance about the TCF and its on-going maintenance. This assurance may include that the taxpayer is transparent with the revenue body and shares the results and follow up actions that flow from the identification of the error and any improvements to the TCF to correct the matter and to also avoid a recurrence.

Revenue bodies do not provide sign off on how the tax return is produced, and they are not obliged to say anything formal about the tax compliance process within the business. They can provide some assurance or satisfaction by discussing the use of internal and/or external audit functions, for example by discussing whether any aspect of the tax return requires more attention or whether an audit is appropriate. Dialogue between a taxpayer and a revenue body about the operation of the TCF can yield positive outcomes for both parties including improvements to the TCF.

Revenue bodies will also need to apply some audit resources even to taxpayers who appear to be low risk, in order to:

- validate the reliability of their testing methods used in evaluating the adequacy of a TCF
- help sustain the integrity of the tax system; and deter taxpayers from attempting to gain an unfair advantage by presenting a false, low-risk picture.

Notes

1. See page 58.

Chapter 4

Conclusions and recommendations

This chapter sets out the conclusions, recommendations and next steps.

The TCF Countries' compliance management strategies of their large business taxpayer population segment have to operate within the broader context of each country's tax system, administrative practice and culture. Not all countries participating in the development of this report have implemented the cooperative compliance concept. Countries that have adopted the concept have modified it to fit the specifics of their own country. It is against this background that this report reaches the following conclusions and recommendations.

Conclusions

- The value to both a taxpayer and the tax administration of a fully developed and monitored internal control system that includes a robust tax control framework is well demonstrated.
- A common understanding about a TCF, its essential features and how it is deployed in practice underpins the successful operation of a co-operative compliance relationship.
- In circumstances where both parties have agreed to be transparent, a fully developed TCF provides a verifiable assurance to the taxpayer and the revenue body that tax risks generally may not arise because of a lack of control and a poor understanding of the tax risks on the part of the enterprise itself.
- Although it is not possible to prescribe a one-size-fits-all system of internal control, six principles or essential building blocks were identified. They are: tax strategy established; applied comprehensively; responsibility assigned; governance documented; testing performed; and assurance provided.
- To form an opinion on the effectiveness of a particular TCF, the revenue body needs to assess and test its scope and effectiveness.
- Revenue bodies may also have mandatory disclosure regimes designed to ensure disclosure of tax risks to obtain greater assurance about the reliability of an enterprises tax risk management system.
- To assure external stakeholders that the revenue body is impartial, tax officials must remain impartial and professional to retain a critical attitude towards the taxpayer and the information and tax risks that it discloses.

Recommendations

Based on these conclusions, and building on the work of the Large Business Programme and of the Forum on Tax Administration, this report recommends that:

1. In relation to member countries concerned about evaluating the risk management systems, structures and policies of businesses that have committed to engage in a co-operative compliance relationship they should:

   – Review the content of this report with a view to evaluating how these TCFs can best be assessed

- Leverage TCFs to continue finding ways to strengthen the cooperative compliance model through effective management of compliance risks including providing certainty in exchange for transparency

2. In relation to evaluating risk management systems, this report recommends that FTA countries:

   - Formulate their own methods of evaluating businesses risk management systems

3. In relation to obtaining greater assurance about the reliability of these systems from a tax perspective this report recommends that FTA countries:

   - Evaluate the merits of issuing additional guidance designed to ensure the disclosure of tax risks

Next Steps

LBP member countries will continue to share experiences with TCFs to assist in creating a compliance framework that benefits both tax administrations and taxpayers. The LBP may revisit this topic in two or three years to learn about countries' experience and best practices.

Bibliography

Financial Accounting Standards Board (FASB) (2008), Statement of Financial Accounting Concepts No. 2, *Qualitative Characteristics of Accounting Information.* www.fasb.org/cs/BlobServer?blobcol=urldata&blobtable=MungoBlobs&blobkey=id&blobwhere=1175820900526&blobheader=application%2Fpdf

OECD (2008), *Study into Tax Intermediaries*, OECD Publishing, Paris, http://dx.doi.org/10.1787/9789264041813-en.

OECD (2013a), *Co-operative Compliance: A framework – From Enhanced Relationship to Co-operative Compliance*, OECD Publishing, Paris, http://dx.doi.org/10.1787/9789264200852-en.

OECD (2013b), *Action Plan on Base Erosion and Profit Shifting*, OECD Publishing, Paris, http://dx.doi.org/10.1787/9789264202719-en.

OECD (2015a), *Mandatory Disclosure Rules, Action 12 - 2015 Final Report*, OECD/G20 Base Erosion and Profit Shifting Project, OECD Publishing, Paris, http://dx.doi.org/10.1787/9789264241442-en.

OECD (2015b), *Transfer Pricing Documentation and Country-by-Country Reporting, Action 13 - 2015 Final Report*, OECD/G20 Base Erosion and Profit Shifting Project, OECD Publishing, Paris, http://dx.doi.org/10.1787/9789264241480-en.

Annex A

BIAC Statement of Tax Principles for International Business

Intention of statement of tax principles - September 2013 (http://biac.org/pdf)

This Statement of Tax Principles is intended to promote and affirm responsible business tax management by international business. These principles are based on five key observations:

- Public trust in the tax system is a vital part of any flourishing society and growing economy.
- Most businesses comply fully with all applicable tax laws and regulations, recognising the obligations of governments to protect a sustainable tax base.
- International businesses contribute significantly to the global economy and pay a substantial amount of tax comprising not only corporation tax, but also labour taxes, social contributions and other taxes such as environmental levies and VAT.
- Transparency, open dialogue and co-operation between tax authorities and business contributes to greater compliance and a better functioning tax system.
- Tax is a business expense which needs to be managed, like any other, and therefore businesses may legitimately respond to tax incentives and statutory alternatives offered by governments.

The objectives

- To enhance co-operation, trust and confidence between tax authorities, business taxpayers and the public in regard to the operation of the global tax system.
- To promote the efficient working of the tax system to fund public services and promote sustainable growth.
- To support stability, certainty and consistency in global tax principles that will foster cross-border trade and investment.

Tax planning principles

- International businesses should only engage in tax planning that is aligned with commercial and economic activity and does not lead to an abusive result.
- International businesses may respond to tax incentives and exemptions.
- International businesses should interpret the relevant tax laws in a reasonable way, consistent with a relationship of 'co-operative compliance' with tax authorities.
- In international tax matters, businesses should follow the terms of the applicable Double Taxation Treaties and relevant domestic and OECD guidance. Business should engage constructively in international dialogue on the review of global tax rules and the need for any changes.

Transparency and reporting principles

Relationships between international businesses and tax authorities should be transparent, constructive, and based on mutual trust with the result that tax authorities and business should treat each other with respect, and with an appropriate focus on areas of risk. International businesses should, therefore:

- Be open and transparent with the tax authority in each jurisdiction about their tax affairs and provide the relevant, reasonably requested information (subject to appropriate confidentiality provisions) that is necessary to enable a reasonable review of possible tax risk.
- Work collaboratively with tax authorities to achieve early agreement on disputed issues and certainty on a real- time basis, wherever possible.
  - Seek, where necessary, to increase public understanding in the tax system in order to build public trust in that system, and, to that end:
  - Where they determine such explanations would be helpful to building public trust in the tax system, they should consider how best to explain to the public their economic contribution and taxes paid in the jurisdictions in which they operate.

Annex B

Select OECD FTA publications of relevance

1. Co-operative Compliance: A Framework. From Enhanced Relationship to Co-operative Compliance, 2013 (May)

http://www.oecd.org/ctp/administration/co-operative-compliance.htm

In 2008, the FTA completed a Study into the Role of Tax Intermediaries which recommended that revenue bodies develop a relationship with large businesses based on trust and co-operation. This 2013 report on co-operative compliance is based on a detailed examination of the practical experiences of several countries since that was study was conducted. It finds that the original recommendation remains valid but identifies additional features that are key to successful "co-operative compliance" strategies. The report addresses the compatibility of the approach with certain legal principles and the internal governance of these programmes within revenue bodies. The importance of making a sound business case for the approach and how to measure the results are discussed. The report concludes with some thoughts about the future direction of the co-operative compliance concept.

***2. Guidance Note* - Guidance and Specifications for Tax Compliance of Business and Accounting Software** (GASBAS), 2010 (April)

www.oecd.org/dataoecd/42/33/45045404.pdf

This guidance note describes in general terms the standards that should be applied in the development of tax accounting software and the key controls that are expected from a tax perspective. It sets out the high-level design principles covering the processes found in a typical computerized business accounting system, including the integration of internal and tax protection controls; procedures to ensure the reliability of electronic records; and the facility to export data for further analysis. It also demonstrates how tax audit processes can be carried out with greater reliability and in such a way that costs to both revenue authorities and businesses can be minimized, and provides guidance on how the principles may be implemented in practice.

***3. Guidance Note* - Guidance on Test Procedures for Tax Audit Assurance**, 2010 (April)

www.oecd.org/dataoecd/42/34/45045414.pdf

This guidance note contains a detailed inventory of compliance and substantive tests performed by tax auditors that could also be performed by businesses to check the operation of their internal controls. It describes the tests that revenue bodies would expect in the control activities and monitoring component of the internal control framework.

4. Information Note - **Tax Compliance and Tax Accounting Systems,** 2010 (April)

www.oecd.org/dataoecd/42/37/45045662.pdf

The note discusses internal control frameworks for tax and how the adoption by revenue bodies and business of the OECD FTA Guidance Notes on business and accounting software specifications can be an important element of internal control frameworks for tax. The use by a business of an internal control framework for tax will demonstrate a willingness to deal transparently with the revenue body who should reciprocate by providing increased and timely tax certainty.

5. Information Note - **General Administrative Principles: Corporate governance and tax risk management**, 2009 (July)

www.oecd.org/dataoecd/37/19/43239887.pdf

This information note deals with the topic of corporate governance and tax risk management. It shares and builds on the experiences and lessons of three countries, Australia, Canada and Chile in encouraging good corporate governance and continuing to develop approaches to sound tax risk management. Despite these countries' diverse regulatory environments and experiences they suggest a number of common benefits, challenges, and best practice considerations.

6. Study into the Role of Tax Intermediaries, 2008 (January)

www.oecd.org/dataoecd/28/34/39882938.pdf

This report describes the key findings and recommendations of the study and focuses on the objective of achieving an 'enhanced relationship' between revenue bodies, taxpayers and tax intermediaries.

The study's key finding is that revenue bodies could achieve a more effective and efficient relationship in their dealings with taxpayers and tax intermediaries if their actions are based upon the following attributes: 1) Understanding based on commercial awareness; 2) Impartiality; 3) Proportionality; 4) Openness; and 5) Responsiveness. These attributes are fundamental for any revenue body and should underpin all their dealings with taxpayers. If revenue bodies demonstrate these five attributes and have effective risk-management processes in place, large corporate taxpayers would be more likely to engage in a relationship with revenue bodies based on co-operation and trust, what is described in the report as an "enhanced relationship".

An enhanced relationship offers benefits for revenue bodies as well as taxpayers. The report notes that taxpayers who behave transparently can expect greater certainty and an earlier resolution of tax issues with less extensive audits and lower compliance costs. An enhanced relationship between revenue bodies and tax intermediaries would also yield significant benefits.

ORGANISATION FOR ECONOMIC CO-OPERATION AND DEVELOPMENT

The OECD is a unique forum where governments work together to address the economic, social and environmental challenges of globalisation. The OECD is also at the forefront of efforts to understand and to help governments respond to new developments and concerns, such as corporate governance, the information economy and the challenges of an ageing population. The Organisation provides a setting where governments can compare policy experiences, seek answers to common problems, identify good practice and work to co-ordinate domestic and international policies.

The OECD member countries are: Australia, Austria, Belgium, Canada, Chile, the Czech Republic, Denmark, Estonia, Finland, France, Germany, Greece, Hungary, Iceland, Ireland, Israel, Italy, Japan, Korea, Luxembourg, Mexico, the Netherlands, New Zealand, Norway, Poland, Portugal, the Slovak Republic, Slovenia, Spain, Sweden, Switzerland, Turkey, the United Kingdom and the United States. The European Union takes part in the work of the OECD.

OECD Publishing disseminates widely the results of the Organisation's statistics gathering and research on economic, social and environmental issues, as well as the conventions, guidelines and standards agreed by its members.

OECD PUBLISHING, 2, rue André-Pascal, 75775 PARIS CEDEX 16
(23 2016 15 1 P) ISBN 978-92-64-25398-8 – 2016

www.ingramcontent.com/pod-product-compliance
Lightning Source LLC
LaVergne TN
LVHW081424110826
845149LV00010B/1860

* 9 7 8 9 2 6 4 2 5 3 9 8 8 *